YOUR KNOWLEDGE HAS VALUE

- We will publish your bachelor's and master's thesis, essays and papers

- Your own eBook and book - sold worldwide in all relevant shops

- Earn money with each sale

Upload your text at www.GRIN.com
and publish for free

Bibliographic information published by the German National Library:

The German National Library lists this publication in the National Bibliography; detailed bibliographic data are available on the Internet at http://dnb.dnb.de .

This book is copyright material and must not be copied, reproduced, transferred, distributed, leased, licensed or publicly performed or used in any way except as specifically permitted in writing by the publishers, as allowed under the terms and conditions under which it was purchased or as strictly permitted by applicable copyright law. Any unauthorized distribution or use of this text may be a direct infringement of the author s and publisher s rights and those responsible may be liable in law accordingly.

Imprint:

Copyright © 2018 GRIN Verlag
Print and binding: Books on Demand GmbH, Norderstedt Germany
ISBN: 9783668688643

This book at GRIN:

https://www.grin.com/document/421071

Dexter Roberts

Department of Homeland Security Operational Issues:
Is it Management or Mismanagement?

GRIN Verlag

GRIN - Your knowledge has value

Since its foundation in 1998, GRIN has specialized in publishing academic texts by students, college teachers and other academics as e-book and printed book. The website www.grin.com is an ideal platform for presenting term papers, final papers, scientific essays, dissertations and specialist books.

Visit us on the internet:

http://www.grin.com/

http://www.facebook.com/grincom

http://www.twitter.com/grin_com

Department of Homeland Security Operational Issues:

Is it Management or Mismanagement?

Dexter Roberts

University of Mississippi

- Abstract 2
- Introduction 2
- Financial Mismanagement 2
- Acquisitions 3
- Grant Mismanagement 3
- Transportation Security Agency 4
- Customs and Border Protection 5
- Cyber Security Division of DHS 6
- Employee Misconduct 6
- Recommendations 7
- References 8

The Department of Homeland Security Issues

Abstract

America continues to face major security threats from external and even more from internal threats. The Department of Homeland Security was founded in 2002, following the 9/11 terrorist attacks, with the purpose of ensuring the safety of the nation against all threats foreign and domestic. However, the agency has been faced with issues that seem to derail them their mission. Accusations of financial, personnel, and program mismanagement have led to the loss of billions of dollars, inefficiency in key departments, in addition to mismanagement in various agencies under its umbrella, including FEMA, TSA, and CBP. This paper will analyze the Department of Homeland Security and its components, discuss some of the issues that plague the agency, and offer a solution to counter these issues.

Introduction

The legal justification for the Department of Homeland Security (DHS), can be found in Article 1 Section 8 and in Article 4 Section 4 of the US Constitution. This agency was established in 2002 through the Homeland Security Act, Public Law 107 - 296, by amending the Inspector General Act of 1978. The current concept of the DHS came into existence after the 9/11 terrorist attacks on the United States. What followed was the formation of a unified department that was devoted to ensuring the safety of America from both foreign and domestic threats, as well as to pull resources together to facilitate a more secure nation through secure borders, stronger aviation security, key critical infrastructure protection, and the integration of law enforcement agencies to facilitate the sharing of information amongst these agencies. However, despite the critical role the Department of Homeland Security plays in the national security arena, this agency has been plagued with accusations of financial and program mismanagement, including wasteful spending of taxpayer funds.

Financial Mismanagement

Since its Inception in 2002, the Department of Homeland Security's allocated funds have increased significantly from $29.1 billion in 2003 to $44.3 billion in 2017 (Inserra, 2017). There has been strong criticism over the use of these funds, which include fraud, mismanagement of funds, wasteful spending, and ineffective use of resources, as well as a lack of transparency and excessive bureaucracy. Following an audit by the Department of Homeland Security's Inspector General, two of the major concerns listed were inefficiency in acquisitions and grant mismanagement by FEMA. The Inspector General's office provides independent oversight, investigations, inspections, and audits on the department's programs, operations, and finances. The office also recommends the best ways for the Department of Homeland Security to function effectively and efficiently.

Acquisitions

Acquisitions and money management are major concerns for the Inspector General's office. The Department of Homeland Security is involved in the acquisition of assets that facilitate its operations. However, the IG's office has noted major issues on how these acquisitions have been carried out. According to Mark, (2015), poor execution of policies has resulted in delays and cost overruns that have mounted to billions of dollars. A report indicated that 14 out of 22 programs in 2015, had schedule delays that resulted in ballooning costs by an estimated $9.7 billion dollars (Rockwell, 2015), resulting in wasteful expenditure of resources. Director of acquisitions insourcing management at GAO, Government Accountability Office, Michael Maclin notes that "the department's acquisition policies are sound and only the execution of the policies has led to some of the issues raised." Maclin attributes the lack of implementation to three major factors: the lack of adequate personnel to execute the policies on a daily basis, the mismatch of budgeting needs vs what is allocated to the DHS, and lastly, last minute or mid-course changes of various programs that lead to increased cost (Rockwell, 2015).

For example, in 2012, the Department of Homeland Security spent $36 million purchasing vehicles that were hardly used. In addition, the US Customs and Border Protection Agency spent a whopping $17 million on a housing project in Arizona, while millions of dollars of mobile homes that were previously purchased sat unused (Ehley, 2014). The DHS's programs and lack of management execution are continuously faced with issues of schedule delays and failure to meet deadlines, costing the agency millions of dollars.

Grant Mismanagement

The Department of Homeland Security has struggled to administer grants and keep track of where the money issued goes. FEMA, Federal Emergency Management Agency, under the umbrella of DHS, is responsible for managing the federal government's response to and recovery from all disaster incidents domestically. In addition, FEMA is responsible for coordinating programs that prevent, mitigate, respond, and recover during a disaster. To perform this role, the agency awards an estimated $10 billion each year to support disaster assistance and preparedness in different areas. However, despite the role that FEMA plays administering and managing federal grants, it has remained a troubling issue for the DHS (Roth, 2017). The lack of the agency's ability to hold grantees accountable and oversight of the federal grants program has led to the ineffectiveness and inefficient management of a program that allocates billions of dollars in federal aid. This issue leaves the program vulnerable to fraud, abuse, and wasteful spending.

In 2016, a report by the Inspector General's office established that out of the $1.5 billion issued as grants in 2015, $457 million was used questionably for things like duplicate payments, unorthodox procurement processes, and unauthorized expenditures, among others (Office of Inspector General, 2015). An audit on the entire grants program called into question an estimated $3 billion, which represents 29% of the grants allocated (Office of Inspector General, 2015). This is higher than the industry norm and a clear indication of a lack of management.

The problems with this program can be attributed to two factors;

1. The lack of oversight of the grants program and the failure to implement policies and procedures that have a stringent amount of controls to balance the finances versus expenditures of the grants program.
2. The laxity of program managers to hold the grant recipients financially accountable for improper and unauthorized usage of the disaster relief funds. As of 2016, FEMA is not taking significant actions on the 24 recommendations of the $413 million the Office of the Attorney General has disallowed as not spent properly (Roth, 2017).

Transportation Security Agency

TSA, Transportation Security Agency, CBP, Customs and Border Patrol, and CSD, Cyber Security Division, are all under the umbrella of the Department of Homeland Security. The TSA was formed in the wake of the 9/11 attacks. Its primary mission is to protect and secure the nation's transportation system, as well as, facilitate free movement of people and trade. One of the measures put in place to ensure the safety of air travel is mandatory screenings before flights. However, in recent times, undercover test have found that TSA screeners failed to detect drugs, knives, and other weapons including explosives. In 2015, investigations reveal that screeners' failure rate was almost 95%. This revelation was brought to light during a Homeland Security house committee meeting (Brandner, & Marsh, 2015).

These high failure rates put passengers, flight crews, and other stakeholders at risk, because terrorist can easily exploit such a weakness and use it to potentially cause another terrorist incident.

Another major challenge faced by TSA is the long security checkpoints that are a direct result of policies put in place to facilitate safer air travel. Since 2013, the number of screeners has dropped from 47000 to roughly 44900 in 2017. As we see a decline in the number of screeners that TSA employees, there is also an influx in passengers of about 15% annually. This balloons the passenger to screener ratio and increases wait times for each passenger passing through security checkpoints.

In addition to security checkpoints, the TSA has been plagued with reports of low morale and high attrition rates amongst screeners. This is a direct result of high turnovers in leadership and repeated misconduct of senior managers (Harrington, 2017). Every major airport in the country experiences long security checkpoints and this has led to passenger inconvenience and wasted time, since passengers must arrive at the airport two to three hours prior to their flight departure to make sure that security checkpoints are cleared in ample time to make their flight (McGeehan, & Nixon, 2016).

Customs and Border Protection

The Customs and Border Protection Agency is an agency within the Department of Homeland Security that secures the United States borders from illegal movement of drugs, contraband, people, and weapons from entering the country illegally, while at the same time, facilitating lawful entry and exit of people and goods. Despite the amount of resources allocated to research and technologies to secure our sovereign borders, there have been concerns over the failure to distinguish between dangerous and safe goods, as well as, travelers with ill-intent. The U.S. borders have seen an influx of drugs and illegal immigrants into the country. These traveler loopholes can be used to facilitate a threat on U.S. soil, as well as, smuggling contraband into the country, and supporting human trafficking across borders.

In 2017, the Office of the Inspector General, released a report on mismanagement at the Customs and Border Protection Agency. One key issue observed was the lack of identifying the effectiveness of the Border Security Programs enacted by the CBP and whether these expensive programs were actually working. Nevertheless, continuous investment of resources without a quantifiable knowledge of whether these programs are effective, has possibly led to billions of allocated resources wasted, and a potentially unsecured border protection program that is highly susceptible to the exploits of terrorists, drug traffickers, and illegal immigrants.

Cyber Security Division of DHS

The Cyber Security Division handles any cyber issues that fall within the authority of the Department of Homeland Security. The responsibilities of this agency have continued to expand since digital technology and internet evolution continues to trend. With malicious criminal internet activity, espionage, and hacktivism threatening the security of the country's government agencies, financial sector, and critical infrastructure, it was important to enhance the information infrastructure by delivering new tools and technologies to mitigate and secure these systems against future attacks (Cyber Security Division, 2018).

Nevertheless, the Cyber Security Division of the Department of Homeland Security has major problems and grave shortcomings as reported by a federal oversight report (Coburn, 2015). The report entails that the Cyber Security Division struggles to execute its responsibilities, strategies, and programs, and is unlikely to protect us from adversaries that pose a serious threat (Coburn, 2015). The report also alludes to: critical security updates not being performed, using vulnerable software and systems, and poor execution of operational actions (Coburn, 2015).

With the recent implication of Russia's actions concerning the 2016 Presidential election, the actions of this agency could potentially lead to another cyber intrusion that has national security implications. The Department of Homeland Security and the Cyber Security Division need to overhaul its agency's management staff and security measures to reduce vulnerabilities in critical infrastructure from possible cyber threats.

Employee Misconduct

The systems put in place by the Department of Homeland Security are meant to reinforce our safety. However, these systems can only work towards detecting and eliminating the threat, if the people who have a responsibility to implement them do so with integrity and honor. In major departments of the DHS, there have been allegations of employee misconduct. This type of behavior erodes the public's confidence in the system and jeopardizes the safety and security of the nation. Recently, a U.S. Majority Staff of the House of Homeland Security Committee report accused TSA employees of misconduct and poor management. It alleges that nearly half of those employed were involved in misconduct between 2013 and 2017 (Perry & Katko, 2016). These allegations include: Theft, drug trafficking, accepting bribes, sexual misconduct, and solicitation of prostitutes. Scott Perry was quoted saying "the level of threats facing America due to TSA's lack of accountability and misconduct is unacceptable and alarming" (Perry & Katko, 2016).

Other accusations include: FEMA hiring employees with criminal backgrounds and in the process incurring a $350,000 expenditure, CBP's possible civil rights violations, and DHS for taking bribes. The office of the Inspector General confirmed that it is investigating potential abuse on constitutional and civil rights of people detained by the Customs and Border Protection Agency, under the implementation of President Trump's executive order for a travel ban (Pilkington, 2017). A 2017 report also accuses DHS employees of taking over $15 million in bribes. Although the number of employees accused of these allegations represent 1% of the DHS staff, according to the office of the Inspector General, any amount less than 100% is not acceptable.

Recommendations

After more than a decade of existence, the Department of Homeland Security continues to face operational challenges, just like any other normal organization. However, these weaknesses can be a major risk to our national security if the existing loopholes are not sealed. More resources are needed in; staffing departments, checks and balances to tackle grant mismanagement, long security checkpoints at the airports, and accountability in the Cyber Security Division.

The hiring process for agency employees should be more stringent; applicants should always be thoroughly vetted, to weed out any criminal elements that may corrode the integrity of the agencies. Allegations of corruption, bribery, and employee misconduct should be investigated by an independent oversight body to ensure the responsible individuals are held accountable for any illegal actions committed. After 15 years, the state of our country's security infrastructure is in a deplorable state. There needs to be a critical overhaul in some departments, investment in critical infrastructures, and the mandatory retraining of employees to include yearly recertification of key positions. This will enhance our capacity to evaluate employee competency and eliminate any potential security threats.

References

Boyd, A. (2018, February 07). *DHS Needs More Cybersecurity Workers-It Just Doesn't Know Where Or What Kind.* Retrieved March 17, 2018, from http://www.nextgov.com/cio-briefing/2018/02/dhs-needs-more-cybersecurity-workersit-just-doesnt-know-where-or-what-kind/145802/

Bradner, E., & Marsh, R. (2015, June 2). *Acting TSA director reassigned after screeners failed tests to detect explosives, weapons.* CNN. Retrieved March 17, 2018, from https://edition.cnn.com/2015/06/01/politics/tsa-failed-undercover-airport-screening-tests/index.html

Ehley, B. (2014, November 26). *68 Ways Homeland Security Has Wasted Your Tax Dollars.* Retrieved March 07, 2018, from http://www.thefiscaltimes.com/2014/11/26/68-Ways-Homeland-Security-Has-Wasted-Your-Tax-Dollars

Harrington, E. (2017, March 03). *Report: Border Security Programs Riddled With Mismanagement.* Retrieved March 17, 2018, from http://freebeacon.com/national-security/report-border-security-programs-riddled-mismanagement/

Inserra, D. (2017). *Congress must re-set department of homeland security priorities: American lives depend on it.* Retrieved from https://www.heritage.org/homeland-security/report/congress-must-re-set-department-homeland-security-priorities-american

Kahan, J. H. (2013). What's in a name? The meaning of homeland security. *Journal of Homeland Security Education, 2,* 1.

McGeehan, P., & Nixon, R. (2016, May 27). *Behind Long Airport Lines, a Chain of T.S.A. Cuts, Missteps and Crises.* The New York Times. Retrieved March 17, 2018, from https://www.nytimes.com/2016/05/28/us/politics/tsas-long-lines-were-avoidable-travelers-and-experts-say.html

Nixon, R. (2016, December 2016). *Homeland Security agents took $15M in bribes, closed their eyes.* The Seattle Times. Retrieved March 17, 2018, from https://www.seattletimes.com/nation-world/homeland-security-agents-took-15m-in-bribes-closed-their-eyes/

Office of Inspector General. (2015). *Summary and key findings of fiscal year 2015 FEMA disaster grant and program audits.* Retrieved from https://www.oig.dhs.gov/sites/default/files/assets/2017/OIG-17-13-D-Dec16.pdf

Perry, S., & Katko, J. (2016, July 7). *Committee releases new TSA misconduct report - house committee on homeland security.* Retrieved from https://homeland.house.gov/press/committee-releases-new-tsa-misconduct-report/

Pilkinton, E. (2017, March 22). *Watchdog investigating DHS for alleged misconduct by immigration officials at airports.* Retrieved March 17, 2018, from https://www.theguardian.com/us-news/2017/mar/22/us-immigration-investigation-misconduct-airports-travel-ban

Rockwell, M. (2015, April 23). *Trouble tracking DHS acquisition.* Retrieved March 07, 2018, from https://fcw.com/articles/2015/04/23/tracking-dhs-acquisition.aspx

Roth, J. (2017, February 15). *High Risk: Government Operations Susceptible to Waste, Fraud, and Mismanagement.* Interview by Committee on Homeland Security and Governmental Affairs. Retrieved from https://www.hsgac.senate.gov/imo/media/doc/Testimony-Roth-2017-02-15.pdf

YOUR KNOWLEDGE HAS VALUE

- We will publish your bachelor's and
  master's thesis, essays and papers

- Your own eBook and book -
  sold worldwide in all relevant shops

- Earn money with each sale

Upload your text at www.GRIN.com
and publish for free